Komodo Dragons
AND Geckos

Henry Thatcher

PowerKiDS press
New York

Published in 2014 by The Rosen Publishing Group, Inc.
29 East 21st Street, New York, NY 10010

First Edition

Produced for Rosen by Cyan Candy, LLC
Editor: Joshua Shadowens
Designer: Erica Clendening, Cyan Candy

Photo Credits: All images www.shutterstock.com.

Library of Congress Cataloging-in-Publication Data

Thatcher, Henry, author.
 Komodo dragons and geckos / By Henry Thatcher. — First edition.
    pages cm. — (Big animals, small animals)
 Includes index.
 ISBN 978-1-4777-6106-9 (library binding) — ISBN 978-1-4777-6107-6 (pbk.) —
 ISBN 978-1-4777-6108-3 (6-pack)
 1. Komodo dragon—Juvenile literature. 2. Geckos—Juvenile literature. 3. Lizards—Juvenile
literature. I. Title.
 QL666.L29T43 2014
 597.95—dc23
                              2013020350

Manufactured in the United States of America

CPSIA Compliance Information: Batch #W14PK2: For Further Information contact Rosen Publishing, New York, New York at 1-800-237-9932

Table of Contents

Lizards Large AND Small

Animals in the lizard family can range widely in size. One of the smallest lizards is a type of gecko that can fit completely on a quarter. The largest living lizard is the Komodo dragon, which can reach nearly 10 feet (3 m) in length.

No matter what their size, lizards share many common **features**. They have scales, legs, and great eyesight. They also differ in many ways, though.

This is a picture of a New Caledonian crested gecko. You can see how small it is compared to a person's fingers.

The scientific name for a Komodo dragon is *Varanus komodoensis*. As you can see, it has long, sharp claws and a very long tail.

BIG FACT!

There are more than 5,600 species, or kinds, of lizards on Earth. That is a lot of lizards!

Some live in trees, while others live on land. Some make their homes in dry deserts, and others like to live in wet, steamy rain forests. Some lizards can change color, and some have sticky toes for climbing.

Let's look at some ways that large Komodo dragons and small geckos are alike and different. Are you ready to find out more?

Where IN THE World?

Lizards can be found on every **continent** on Earth except Antarctica. Geckos live in warm **climates** throughout the world. In the United States they live in southern states, such as Florida, Georgia, and Texas. They are only found in cooler climates when they are kept as pets. Komodo dragons have a more limited range than geckos do. Komodo dragons are found only on the

This curious gecko is sitting on a flower called the torch ginger. Both the gecko and flower can be found in Southeast Asia.

Indonesian islands of Komodo, Rinca, Flores, Gili Motang, and Padar. The Komodo dragons used to have a wider range, but it has gotten much smaller due to human activities. The Komodo dragon **population** has dropped so much that they are now **endangered**. This means they could one day disappear from the Earth! Komodo dragons are also found in many zoos throughout the world.

LONG CLAWS

Home Sweet Home

Geckos may be small, but there sure are a lot of them! There are around 1,500 species of geckos in the world.

The largest species was called the Kawekaweau and lived in New Zealand. It grew to be 24 inches long (60 cm). This gecko is now **extinct**. The largest living species is the New Caledonian giant gecko. It grows to be up to 14 inches (36 cm) long. The smallest gecko species lives on an island off the Dominican Republic.

ALBINO GECKO

This is a giant Madagascar day gecko. They come from Africa, but can make great pets all over the world. This type of gecko is most active in the daytime, unlike most other geckos, so you can watch its movements.

The Dominican Republic is in the Caribbean Sea, south of Florida. This tiny lizard is only 0.6 inches (1.6 cm) long. That's only about as big as an adult's thumbnail!

Geckos live in many habitats. They can be found in rain forests, deserts, mountainsides, or even sharing homes with people. The geckos that live near humans help keep harmful bug populations down.

Here, a Komodo dragon is sunning itself on the small island of Rinca in the South Pacific. It is one of the few places that Komodo dragons naturally live.

The Komodo dragon is a single species related to monitor lizards. Their range is limited to a few volcanic islands in Indonesia. These lizards live in hot, dry places within their island homes. They like dry, open grasslands, savannas, and tropical forests most. They can also be found on the beaches and mountainsides of their island homes. They are the top **predators** in their habitats. They spend the nights and the hottest parts of the day in burrows that are not much larger than the dragons themselves.

Are They Alike?

At first glance, it may be hard to tell how the giant Komodo dragon and tiny geckos might be alike. There are similarities, though. They are both lizards, which means they are also both **reptiles**. Both lizards, and all other lizards in the world, are **ectothermic**, or cold-blooded. They cannot heat or cool their own bodies from within. Their temperature matches that of their surroundings.

Geckos and Komodo dragons also have scales. Geckos scales are not nearly as tough as the Komodo dragons'

The most commonly kept type of pet gecko is the leopard gecko, seen here. One of the ways they differ from most other geckos is that they walk on the ground instead of climbing.

scales. A gecko's skin can easily be torn. Both lizards have tails. Sometimes geckos can drop their tails off to escape predators. Komodo dragons cannot. Lucky for them, they do not have predators!

Lizards are very closely related to snakes. One of the things that distinguishes all lizards, including geckos and Komodo dragons, from snakes is that lizards have external ears. They also have legs. Komodo dragons have long, powerful claws they use to catch prey. Geckos have smaller claws, but they have something Komodo dragons do not. They have very sticky feet.

This Komodo has made its way onto someone's patio. Komodos' saliva is toxic, and sometimes they attack people.

Like snakes, lizards also have an organ in their mouths for picking up smells. They use their tongue to bring in the tiny bits of smell from the air into their mouths. There, the **Jacobson's organ** breaks apart the smell to give information about what animal is nearby, or how long ago it may have passed through.

JACOBSON'S ORGAN

Comparing GECKOS AND

Size (length)	0.6–24 inches (1.6–60 cm)
Habitat	forests, deserts, and others
Diet	insectivores/omnivores
Predators	birds, mammals, and others
Prey	crickets and other insects
Life Span	10–20 years

KOMODO DRAGONS

Size (length)	10 feet (3 m)
Habitat	hot, dry places
Diet	carnivores/omnivores
Predators	none
Prey	snakes, goats, and deer
Life Span	30 years

Largest Living Lizard

Though Komodo dragons have been living on their Indonesian islands for millions of years, people did not discover them until 100 years ago. Since then, scientists have been studying them to find out more about them. They have found that Komodo dragons do not rely on hearing or sight as much as they do on smell to get around and find food. Much like snakes, Komodo dragons use their long forked tongue to pick up smells. They flick out their tongue and

The Komodo dragon is the largest lizard in the world. It has no predators, and is a carnivore. One of a Komodo's favorite prey is deer.

FORKED TONGUE

then carry the smells back into their mouth. If they find a smell that seems like lunch they will track it down and eat the animal they find at the end of the trail.

At lengths of up to 10 feet (3 m), Komodo dragons are the longest lizards on Earth. They are also the heaviest. They weigh in at more than 300 pounds (150 kg). That is a lot of lizard!

Komodos can climb trees using their long, sharp claws. These claws are also helpful in attacking prey.

It also makes it even more surprising that these huge lizards took so long to be found by people.

It might have taken so long to find them because they live in **remote** parts of the world. It could also be because these lizards live in harsh climates where many other animals could not survive. They live in places that have little

Komodo dragons can roam the beaches of the islands they inhabit with no threats since they have no animal predators.

rainfall, intense heat, and active volcanic activity. Luckily, Komodo dragons are excellent swimmers. If conditions become too harsh where they are, they can swim to a neighboring island.

Amazing Geckos

Geckos are some of the most colorful lizards in the world. Different species have their own unique coloration and patterns on their skin. Some geckos can even change color, becoming lighter in color at night. As with all reptiles, geckos shed their skin as they grow. This is called molting. Geckos help get rid of their old skins by eating them.

STICKY TOES

Geckos are known for their amazing, sticky feet. They can walk easily up walls and across ceilings. They can do this because their toes have a special adaptation. Each toe is covered in millions of hairlike parts. These hairlike parts each have between 100 and 1,000 spatula-shaped parts at their ends. Through a tricky bit of science all these tiny cells let the gecko stick to most surfaces. The stickiness is so powerful it could support two adult humans!

 This gargoyle gecko, or New Caledonian bumpy gecko, is only found on the island of New Caledonia.

This green gecko is sitting on a beautiful bird of paradise flower in Hawaii. Green geckos live all over the world.

Many species of gecko, including the tokay gecko, can drop off parts of their tail when needed. This can be done to break free from or confuse a predator. The tail piece thrashes and moves for a few minutes. It takes about three weeks for the gecko to regrow its tail. The new tail is generally not as long as the original one.

This Auckland green gecko is about to lick its eyeball to keep it wet and clean.

Geckos have an excellent sense of smell. They smell through their nostrils. They also use their tongue to bring smells inside their mouth to a special part called the Jacobson's organ. Many reptiles have this organ.

Diets: Big AND Small

Komodo dragons start out life living in trees and eating mostly geckos. As they grow, Komodo dragons move to the ground. There, they eat snakes, goats, pigs, and deer. They also eat **carrion**. As they grow to full size, Komodo dragons can hunt and kill large mammals, such as water buffalo.

The Komodo dragon uses its sharp teeth and claws to hunt. It lies in wait, **camouflaged** in it surroundings.

When **prey** passes by it springs and bites the prey. If the animal does not die right away, the Komodo dragon uses its sense of smell to follow the animal. The mouth of a Komodo dragon has more than 50 kinds of bacteria. Within 24 hours, most prey will die from infection and the Komodo will have its dinner.

Komodo dragons use their 60 sharp teeth to bite prey. They will go through up to five sets of teeth in their lifetimes.

BIG FACT!

Komodo dragons can eat up to 80 percent of their body weight in one meal. That is as much as 240 pounds (109 kg) of food.

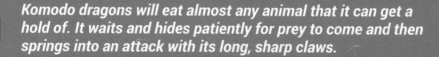

Komodo dragons will eat almost any animal that it can get a hold of. It waits and hides patiently for prey to come and then springs into an attack with its long, sharp claws.

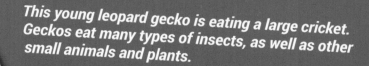

This young leopard gecko is eating a large cricket. Geckos eat many types of insects, as well as other small animals and plants.

When geckos are not being eaten by young Komodos, they are hiding or hunting dinner of their own. Many species of gecko are insectivores. An insectivore is a type of carnivore that eats mainly insects. These might include crickets, grasshoppers, flies, and moths. Some geckos will also eat spiders, fruits, nectar, and small animals. They use their eyesight and sense of smell to track down prey. Most geckos' skin color and patterns help them blend in with their surroundings. This helps them stay safe. It also helps them sneak up on breakfast!

CRICKET

Big or Small, Which is Better?

If a gecko and a Komodo dragon were put into a boxing ring, which one would come out as the champion? In that particular situation, the giant Komodo dragon would likely come out on top. However, in the real world, it is harder to say whether being large or small is better.

The large Komodo dragon is the top predator in its habitat. Geckos, on the other hand, serve as an important

food source for many animals, including Komodo dragons, birds, and mammals.

Yet, Komodo dragons are a single species whose habitat is growing smaller all the time. There are only a few thousand Komodo dragons left in the world. There are more than a thousand species of geckos, and while some are endangered, there are millions of geckos living around the world. So, what do you think? Is it better to be large and in charge or small and adaptable?

Geckos make fun and easy pets. If you own a gecko, make sure to have your parents help so you can take care of it the right way.

Komodo dragons do not make good pets. They are far too dangerous.

Glossary

camouflaged (KA-muh-flahzd) Hidden by looking like the things around one.

carrion (KAR-ee-un) Dead, rotting flesh.

climates (KLY-mits) The kinds of weather certain places have.

continent (KON-tuh-nent) One of Earth's seven large landmasses.

ectothermic (ek-tuh-THER-mik) Having a body heat that changes with the surroundings.

endangered (in-DAYN-jerd) In danger of no longer living.

extinct (ik-STINGKT) No longer existing.

features (FEE-churz) The special looks or forms of people or objects.

Jacobson's organ (JAY-kub-sunz OR-gun) A kind of sensory organ that helps lizards' and snakes' sense of smell and taste.

population (pop-yoo-LAY-shun) A group of animals or people living in the same area.

predators (PREH-duh-terz) Animals that kill other animals for food.

remote (rih-MOHT) Far away.

reptiles (REP-tylz) Cold-blooded animals with lungs and scales.

Index

Websites

Due to the changing nature of Internet links, PowerKids Press has developed an online list of websites related to the subject of this book. This site is updated regularly. Please use this link to access the list: www.powerkids.com/basa/gecko/